101
Annoying Things

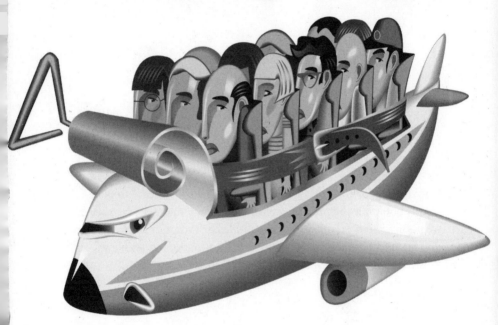

About Air Travel

Ray Comfort

First Printing: March 2007

ISBN-13: 978-0-89221-669-7
ISBN-10: 0-89221-669-7
Library of Congress Catalog Number: 2006937544
Cover design by Janell Robertson.

Printed in the United States of America.

New Leaf Press
A Division of New Leaf Publishing Group

Turbulence that is so bad, the flight attendant puts the food straight into the sick sacks.

Full overhead lockers and nowhere to put your bag.

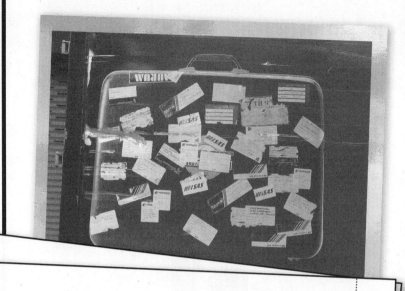

RIDDLES

WHAT IS IT THAT WALKS ALL DAY ON ITS HEAD?

STAND
I

....
MIND-BENDERS

A NAIL IN A HORSESHOE;
I UNDERSTAND

A four-foot wide newspaper in a two-foot seat space.

THE MORE OF THEM YOU TAKE, THE MORE YOU LEAVE BEHIND. WHAT ARE THEY?

"Americans who travel abroad for the first time are often shocked to discover that, despite all the progress that has been made in the last 30 years, many foreign people still speak foreign languages." — Dave Barry

Muffled announcements.

The insistence of airlines to call your destination a "terminal."

MIND-BENDERS

FACED

" "

WHEN IT IS FASTENED, IT WALKS. WHEN IT IS UNFASTENED, IT STOPS. WHAT IS IT?

TWO FACED; A SANDAL.

Gorilla baggage handlers.

Let Lying Dogs Sleep

Two women from Southern California were about to cross the Mexican border to return to the United States when they saw what looked like a very small sick animal in the ditch beside their car. As they examined it in the darkness of the night, they saw that it was a tiny Chihuahua. There and then they decided to take it back to the United States and nurse it back to health. However, because they were afraid that they were breaking the law, they put it in the trunk of their car and drove across the border. Once they were in the States, they retrieved the animal and nursed it until they arrived home.

One of the women was so concerned for the ailing dog she actually took it to bed with her, and reached out at different intervals during the night to touch the tiny animal, and reassure it that she was still present.

The dog was so sick the next morning that she decided to take it to the veterinarian. That's when she found out that the animal wasn't a tiny sick dog. It was a Mexican water rat, dying of rabies.

WHAT IS IT THAT GOES AROUND WOOD BUT NEVER GOES INTO IT?

THE BARK OF A TREE.

Lost baggage.

Food carts that scrape your fingers.

KNEE LIGHTS

I LIVE ALONE IN A VERY SMALL HOUSE. IT HAS NO DOORS OR WINDOWS. IF I WANT TO GO OUT, I HAVE TO BREAK THROUGH THE WALL. WHAT AM I?

NEON LIGHTS, A CHICK INSIDE AN EGG.

Food carts that block your course to the restroom.

POKE YOUR FINGERS INTO ME AND I WILL OPEN MY JAWS. I AM GREEDY TO DEVOUR PAPER AND MATERIALS. WHAT AM I?

Expensive New Van

A Michigan radio station reported the following hunting incident. Two men decided to go duck hunting on a frozen lake. They loaded their $30,000 new van (which was costing them $400 in monthly payments) with their dog, guns, and snacks. They then drove onto the ice, and decided that they would blast a hole in it to place their decoys to attract ducks. Of course, they moved far away from their expensive new van, lit the fuse of a stick of dynamite, and threw it onto the ice. It was then that their highly trained dog ran after the dynamite. The men panicked, waved their arms, and yelled at the dog. The animal, cheered on by their cries, picked up the dynamite, and ran toward them. One of the men grabbed his gun and shot at the dog. The animal became confused and ran under the $30,000 van with the dynamite still in its mouth. The van didn't make it.

SCISSORS.

Lilliputian pillows.
(the pillows are smaller than the word lilliputian)

Aisles designed to be slightly narrower than the width of the bag you are carrying.

IF YOU HAVE IT, YOU PROBABLY WANT TO SHARE IT, BUT IF THE MOMENT YOU SHARE IT, YOU DON'T HAVE IT. WHAT IS IT?

IF TWO'S COMPANY, AND THREE'S A CROWD, THEN WHAT ARE FOUR AND FIVE?

Oversold flights.

HOW MANY TIMES CAN YOU SUBTRACT THE NUMBER 5 FROM 25?

"The cool thing about being famous is traveling. I have always wanted to travel across seas, like to Canada and stuff." – Britney Spears

Delayed flights.

Canceled flights.

AS I WAS GOING TO ST. IVES, I MET A MAN WITH SEVEN WIVES, THE SEVEN WIVES HAD SEVEN SACKS, THE SEVEN SACKS HAD SEVEN CATS, THE SEVEN CATS HAD SEVEN KITTENS; KITTENS, CATS, SACKS, AND WIVES, HOW MANY WERE GOING TO ST. IVES?

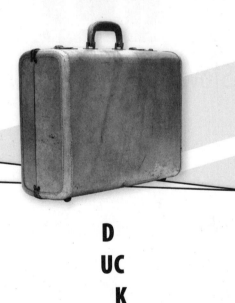

D
UC
K

MIND-BENDERS

ONE. IT DOESN'T SAY THAT THE PEOPLE HE MET WERE GOING TO ST. IVES; SITTING DUCK.

Slow baggage handlers.

I CAN SIZZLE LIKE BACON, I AM MADE WITH AN EGG, I HAVE PLENTY OF BACKBONE, BUT I LACK A GOOD LEG, I PEEL LAYERS LIKE ONIONS, BUT STILL REMAIN WHOLE, I CAN BE LONG, LIKE A FLAGPOLE, YET FIT IN A HOLE, WHAT AM I?

Hertz Hurts

A man who took the Hertz Corporation to court is probably regretting his action. He maintained that the car rental company owed him $17.90 as an insurance refund. Instead of calling the company and trying to negotiate for a settlement, he took them to court. He lost the case when the jury sided with Hertz. He had $450,000 in legal fees.

A SNAKE.

The captain who announces, "We hope to have you 'on the ground' in ten minutes."

Announcements from Captain Holler-it, who deliberately waits until you snooze off.

A HORSE IS TIED TIGHTLY TO A 20-FOOT LONG ROPE. THE HORSE WANTS TO GET SOME WATER THAT IS 40 FEET AWAY, AND GETS TO IT EASILY. HOW IS THIS?

THE OTHER END OF THE ROPE ISN'T TIED TO ANYTHING.

Pea soup fog.

NEPAINCK

Illegible tickets.

Escalators that are out of service the day you take your rock collection.

IN WHAT YEAR DID CHRISTMAS DAY AND NEW YEAR'S DAY FALL ON THE SAME YEAR?

MILE MIST

Terminals designed by the Department of Confusion.

"In America there are two classes of travel — first class, and with children." — Robert Benchley

IT STANDS ON ONE LEG WITH ITS HEART IN ITS HEAD. WHAT IS IT?

A CABBAGE.

Lining up on a jet-way that feels like the inside of a working microwave oven.

The nursery flight.

WHAT IS IT THAT YOU WILL BREAK EVERY TIME YOU NAME IT?

WHAT FASTENS TWO PEOPLE YET TOUCHES ONLY ONE?

SILENCE; A WEDDING RING.

Waiting for a week in a "holding lounge."

I AM THE BEGINNING OF SORROW, AND THE END OF SICKNESS. YOU CANNOT EXPRESS HAPPINESS WITHOUT ME, YET I AM IN THE MIDST OF CROSSES. I AM ALWAYS IN RISK, YET NEVER IN DANGER. YOU MAY FIND ME IN THE SUN, BUT I AM NEVER SEEN OUT OF DARKNESS. WHAT AM I?

Horse Sense

Bill Brugman is from Southern California. He is a man's man, with a deep, manly voice. That's why it shouldn't be a surprise to know that he loves horses. If he wasn't a city-dweller, he would be a cowpoke roaming the dusty plains. In fact, Bill once owned a horse.

Some years ago, he decided to take a horseback ride. He took the saddle from his truck, and as the horse stood by a wooden fence, his manly arms easily lifted the heavy saddle onto the back of his steed. With a sense of cool excitement, he pulled the saddle straps tight. Then, with the ease that only an experienced horseman can muster, he mounted the animal and with a firm command, told it to move.

It didn't go anywhere. He had strapped it to the fence.

THE LETTER S.

You arrive late and find
that the plane left on time.

Your first bag comes off the
baggage claim first, and the
second bag comes off last.

SWEARING
BIBLE
BIBLE
BIBLE
BIBLE
BIBLE
BIBLE
BIBLE

WHAT DO THE NUMBERS 11, 69, AND 88 ALL HAVE IN COMMON?

RIDDLES

SWEARING ON A STACK OF
BIBLES; THEY READ THE SAME
UP-SIDE-DOWN.

Terminals that make a crowded New York sidewalk look deserted.

WHAT IS IT THAT CAN PASS BEFORE THE SUN WITHOUT MAKING ANY SHADOW?

"If forced to travel on an airplane, try and get in the cabin with the Captain, so you can keep an eye on him and nudge him if he falls asleep or point out any mountains looming up ahead." — Mike Harding

THE WINDOW.

Plane brakes that sound like they are on their last legs.

An all-night motor-mouth, who sounds like she is speaking to someone who has a hearing problem.

WHAT IS IT THAT CAN BURN THE EYES, YET BE EATEN?

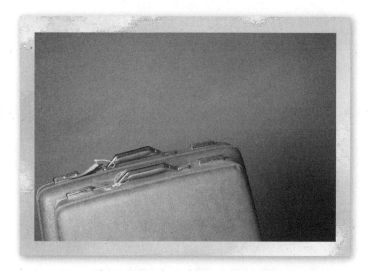

WHAT BOOK WAS ONCE OWNED BY ONLY THE WEALTHY, BUT NOW NEARLY EVERYONE CAN HAVE IT? HOWEVER, YOU CAN'T BUY IT IN A BOOKSTORE OR TAKE IT FROM A LIBRARY?

SALT; A TELEPHONE BOOK.

People who talk about plane crashes when they are taking you to the airport.

R
O
ROADS
D
S

Magazines on sale at airports that have a front-page article about air-traffic controllers sleeping on the job.

Boarding passengers who stand in the aisle and refuse to move while they try and stuff their eight-foot bag into a two-foot overhead bin.

NAME SOMETHING THAT CAN GO UP A CHIMNEY DOWN, BUT CAN'T GO DOWN A CHIMNEY UP?

WHAT'S COLORLESS AND WEIGHTLESS, BUT IF YOU PUT IT INTO A BARREL, THE BARREL WOULD BECOME LIGHTER?

AN UMBRELL, A HOLE.

Exiting passengers who stand in the aisle and won't move when they are trying to pull their eight-foot bag out of the two-foot overhead bin.

WHAT'S BETTER THAN THE BEST THING, AND WORSE THAN THE WORST THING?

Soviet Psychic

A psychic healer from the old Soviet Union tried to use his "powers" to stop a freight train. The train's engineer stated to officials that the psychic, E. Frenkel, stepped onto the tracks with his arms raised, his head lowered, and his body braced.

The Russian newspaper *Sovietskaya Rossiya* reported on October 1 that investigators looking into his decision to jump in front of a train found the answer in the briefcase he left by the side of the tracks. Authorities found notes written by Frenkel in which he alleged, "First I stopped a bicycle, cars, and a streetcar. Now I'm going to stop a train."

Frenkel claimed that halting a train would be the supreme test of his abilities. The train did stop, but only after it had run over him.

NOTHING.

34

Trivial announcements from the flight deck that break in on entertainment.

35

Turbulence that waits until the drinks are poured.

WHAT WON'T BREAK IF YOU THROW IT OFF THE HIGHEST BUILDING IN THE WORLD, BUT WILL BREAK IF YOU PLACE IT IN THE OCEAN?

GETTING

IT ALL

36

Air pockets.

WHAT KIND OF ROCKS ARE ON THE BOTTOM OF THE MISSISSIPPI RIVER?

WET ONES.

Unexplained plane noises.

The Sardine Flight.

WHAT EXACTLY IS KNOWN AS THE CENTER OF GRAVITY?

PRICE

39

Passengers with B.O.
who sit next to you.

NAME SOMETHING THAT HAS NO BEGINNING, END, OR MIDDLE?

High-tech Criminals

Back in 1971, three thieves at Billericay in Essex, England, gave many hours of thought to robbing the local post office on Mountnessing Road. Among the details that they discovered were the times at which there was the most cash and when there were the least security guards on the premises. They also invested in masks, weapons, and a getaway vehicle.

These geniuses left no stone unturned. At a pre-arranged time, the gang sped through the town and screeched to a halt outside the post office. It was only when they jumped out of the car and ran toward the building that they discovered the one detail that they had omitted to check. The post office had been closed for around 12 years.

MAN
BOARD

The 400-pound passenger with a hairy arm that rubs against your bare arm.

Metal detectors that go off at nothing when you are late for a flight.

WHAT HAS A FOOT ON EACH SIDE AND ONE IN THE MIDDLE?

HERE ON EARTH IT IS ALWAYS TRUE, THAT A DAY FOLLOWS A DAY. BUT THERE IS A PLACE WHERE YESTERDAY ALWAYS COMES AFTER TODAY! WHAT AM I?

A YARDSTICK; THE DICTIONARY.

Re-circulated re-circulated air.

One armrest, two arms.

YOUR MOTHER'S BROTHER'S ONLY BROTHER-IN-LAW IS ASLEEP ON YOUR COUCH. WHO IS ASLEEP ON YOUR COUCH?

WHO IS IT THAT CAN SHAVE 25 TIMES A DAY AND STILL HAVE A BEARD?

YOUR FATHER; A BARBER.

The passenger who jolts his seat back during the meal.

**T
O
W
N**

The captain who points out incredible "worth-seeing" sights, on the other side of the plane.

Window shades that get stuck.

WHAT RUNS AROUND A HOUSE BUT DOESN'T MOVE?

WHAT CAN YOU SIT ON, SLEEP ON, AND BRUSH YOUR TEETH WITH?

A FENCE; A CHAIR, A BED, AND A TOOTHBRUSH.

Back row seats that don't go back.

IF ONE CHILD HAS 6 2/3 SAND PILES AND ANOTHER HAS 3 1/3, AND YOU COMBINE THEM, HOW MANY SAND PILES DO YOU HAVE?

"The average airplane is 16 years old, and so is the average airplane meal." — Joan Rivers

ONE.

Pretzels, when you're expecting a meal.

Six-inch high overhead bins.

R E A D I N G

WHAT GOES UP AND NEVER GOES DOWN?

When items fall under your seat with the seatbelt sign on.

Trying to put on a jacket while seated.

WHAT WORD IN THE ENGLISH LANGUAGE IS ALWAYS SPELLED INCORRECTLY?

IF AN ELECTRIC TRAIN IS GOING EAST AT 60 MILES AN HOUR AND THERE IS A STRONG WESTERLY WIND, WHICH WAY DOES THE SMOKE FROM THE TRAIN DRIFT?

INCORRECTLY; AN ELECTRIC TRAIN DOESN'T PRODUCE ANY SMOKE.

Small airports that don't sell food after hours.

Not So Cold Turkey

A man in one of the northern states shot a turkey, and put it and his gun in the trunk of his car. Unfortunately, the turkey wasn't quite dead and it kicked its leg, set off the gun, and the man was shot in the leg.

After he was treated at a local hospital, he was charged for shooting a turkey two weeks before the season began.

SPIEKY

Flight attendants who demonstrate their skills at pouring boiling hot coffee, above your tender skin.

The kid who kicks the seat behind you 800 times a minute.

WHERE DO YOU FIND ROADS WITHOUT VEHICLES, FORESTS WITHOUT TREES, AND CITIES WITHOUT HOUSES?

F
E
E
L
I
N
G
MOUTH

ON A MAP; FEELING DOWN IN THE MOUTH.

People behind you that put their hand on your seat to stand up, and rip out some of your hair as they do so.

WHAT HAS A TONGUE, CANNOT WALK, BUT GETS AROUND A LOT?

A SHOE.

People who walk down the aisle and unwittingly hit you on the head with their carry-on bags.

Kids who run up and down the aisle 2,000 times.

"Too often travel, instead of broadening the mind, merely lengthens the conversation." — *Elizabeth Drew*

WHAT WORD LOOKS THE SAME UPSIDE DOWN AND BACKWARDS?

'SWIMS

Passengers who sit next to you with offensive breath.

Windowless seats.

WHAT HAS FOUR LEGS, A HEAD, AND LEAVES?

CLOU

A DOG THAT IS WALKING AWAY
FROM YOU, PARTLY CLOUDY.

The "good news/bad news"
announcement: "We've arrived
early, but there is another
plane at our gate."

Catastrophic

In 1978, during a firemen's strike in Britain, the army was called in to carry out the normal duties of the firemen. During this time they received a call from a very upset elderly woman, whose cat was stuck up a tree.

The army immediately responded to the woman's call and valiantly rescued the stranded animal. The dear woman was so thrilled that she invited the whole group of soldiers into her home to celebrate the event with tea and cookies.

After the celebration, fond farewells were given. Then off went the army, driving over the cat and killing it.

WHAT HAS WHEELS AND FLIES BUT IS NOT A PLANE?

A TRASH TRUCK.

Inflated airport prices.

Connecting flights with seven seconds between them.

WHAT DO YOU HAVE WHEN 20 RABBITS STEP BACKWARDS?

WHAT AM I? I AM THE ONLY THING THAT ALWAYS TELLS THE TRUTH. I SHOW OFF EVERYTHING THAT I SEE. I COME IN ALL SHAPES AND SIZES.

A RECEDING HARE-LINE; A MIRROR.

Airport gates that are 250 miles apart.

TPMERHOA

"The whole object of travel is not to set foot on foreign land; it is at last to set foot on one's own country as a foreign land." — G.K. Chesterton

Inter-terminal trains which are slower than a dead snail.

The flights from L.A. to San Francisco that fly via Texas, New York, Florida, and Montana.

WHAT HAPPENS TWICE IN A WEEK, AND ONCE IN A YEAR, BUT NEVER IN A DAY?

NAME TWO KEYS THAT UNLOCK NO DOORS.

Ten-mile long check-in lines.

Airports whose parking rates for an hour are more than your car is worth.

WHAT TURNS EVERYTHING AROUND, BUT DOES NOT MOVE?

WHILE WALKING ACROSS A BRIDGE I SAW A BOAT FULL OF PEOPLE. YET THERE WASN'T A SINGLE PERSON ON THE BOAT. WHY?

A MIRROR; ALL THE PASSENGERS ON THE BOAT ARE MARRIED.

Geriatric planes.

O
B.S.
M.S.
PH.D.

"And that's the wonderful thing about family travel: it provides you with experiences that will remain locked forever in the scar tissue of your mind." — Dave Barry

When you have a connecting flight and forget about the time zone change.

Airport taxes.

WHAT FLIES WITHOUT WINGS?

WHAT IS BIGGER WHEN NEW AND GROWS SMALLER WITH USE?

TIME; SOAP.

In-flight flies.

|||||||
0 0

Still Squeamish
Some time ago, some Boeing employees on the field decided to steal a life raft from one of the 747s. They were successful in getting it out of the plant and home. When they took it for a float on the Stilliguamish River, they were quite surprised by a Coast Guard helicopter homing in on the emergency locator that is activated when the raft is inflated.

CIRCLES BENEATH THE EYES.

You find that you are sitting in someone else's seat.

Turbulence while in the bathroom.

YOU CAN DRAW ME, FIRE ME, OR FILL ME IN. WHAT AM I?

RIFLE
RIFLE
RIFLE
RIFLE
RIFLE

A BLANK; REPEATER RIFLE.

Engine reverse thrust that makes the plane shake like the back end of a stirred rattler.

WHAT'S FULL OF HOLES BUT STILL HOLDS WATER?

*"There are only two emotions
in a plane: boredom and terror."*
— Orson Welles

Blankets made of burlap.

Seat belts that you can't locate because they have burrowed their way under the seat cushion.

WHAT HAS EIGHT FINGERS AND TWO THUMBS, BUT IS NOT ALIVE?

HOW MANY LETTERS ARE IN THE ALPHABET?

A PAIR OF GLOVES; THERE ARE ELEVEN (IN THE TWO WORDS).

Airlines that won't tell the "plane" truth about a delayed flight.

HE'S HIMSELF

HE'S BESIDE HIMSELF.

Bursting your face while
trying to "pop" your inner ear
to get rid of an earache.

Being allocated a seat number
that's already taken.

WHAT IS PUT ON A TABLE AND CUT, BUT NEVER EATEN?

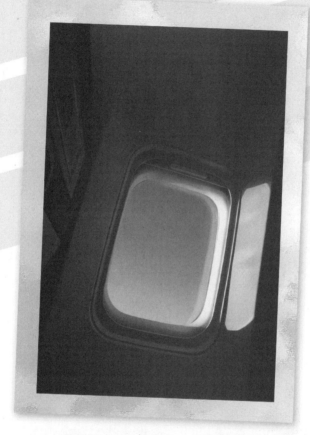

I AM TAKEN FROM A MINE, AND SHUT UP IN A WOODEN CASE, FROM WHICH I AM NEVER RELEASED, AND YET I AM USED BY ALMOST EVERYBODY. WHAT AM I?

PLAYING CARDS; THE LEAD IN A PENCIL.

80

Full overhead lockers and
nowhere to put your bag.

Cracking Smirks

I was running through a New York airport with a very important package in my hand. By the weight of it, it was obviously something of value, so the owner was no doubt going to be *very* pleased when I presented it to him.

About two minutes earlier, I'd noticed the package sticking out from under the seat of a passenger who sat across the aisle from me in the plane. He had obviously forgotten it, and I was the good Samaritan who was taking it to him — I was *running* the extra mile.

After weaving through a mass of human bodies I spun around a corner and saw the man talking with his friends. What a break, to find him among the crowds — *was he going to be pleased with me!*

I boldly interrupted his conversation, held the package out and said, "You left this in the plane." He looked puzzled and said that it wasn't his. It was then that someone remarked, "Oh, that's the rolled up emergency equipment — the life jacket, whistle, etc. It must have fallen from beneath the seat." I could see smirks begin to crack onto a few faces so I backed up and said, "Well . . . it was good to see you again. Bye!" I felt like the Good Samaritan who suddenly found out that the man upon whom he was pouring oil and wine was actually sunbathing.

I made my way back to the plane and with an official air, casually tossed the thing onto the first seat in the plane and walked out.

It was 18 months before I even told a soul what had happened.

WHAT HAS TO BE BROKEN
BEFORE IT CAN BE USED?

AN EGG.

Ice on the wings before takeoff.

When the air-conditioning
gives out.

Z
Z
Z
Z
Z
Z
DOGS

WHAT GROWS WHEN IT EATS, BUT DIES WHEN IT DRINKS?

Being redirected to an
airport a million miles from
where you want to go.

TOUCH
OUT

WHAT DO YOU THROW OUT WHEN YOU WANT TO USE IT, BUT TAKE IN WHEN YOU DON'T WANT TO USE IT?

"I have found out that there ain't no surer way to find out whether you like people or hate them than to travel with them." — Mark Twain

84

Having to walk through first class to get to your "domestic" seat.

85

Mile-long restroom lines.

GUNN, JR.

I AM AROUND LONG BEFORE DAWN.
BUT BY LUNCH I AM USUALLY GONE.
YOU CAN SEE ME SUMMER, FALL,
AND SPRING.
I LIKE TO GET ON EVERYTHING.
BUT WHEN WINTER WINDS START
TO BLOW;
BRR, THEN IT'S TIME FOR ME TO GO!
WHAT AM I?

SONG OF A GUN: MORNING DEW.

Needing to get to the restroom when you are sitting on the inside of sleeping passengers.

"When preparing to travel, lay out all your clothes and all your money. Then take half the clothes and twice the money." — Susan Heller

HE WHO HAS IT DOESN'T TELL ANYONE ABOUT IT. HE WHO TAKES IT DOESN'T KNOW ANYTHING ABOUT IT. HE WHO KNOWS WHAT IT IS DOESN'T WANT TO HAVE ANYTHING TO DO WITH IT. WHAT IS IT?

COUNTERFEIT MONEY.

No paper towels in the restroom.

Having to use the restroom
after turbulence.

THE MORE YOU HAVE OF IT, THE LESS YOU SEE. WHAT IS IT?

PRESSURE

G
N I K
C
A
R
C

DARKNESS; CRACKING UNDER PRESSURE.

Table trays that reveal what passengers for the last two years had for dinner.

WHICH WORD, IF PRONOUNCED RIGHT IS WRONG, BUT IF PRONOUNCED WRONG IS RIGHT?

WRONG.

Passengers who stand up before the plane has stopped at the gate, just after being told to stay seated.

Trying to sleep sitting upright.

READ EACH LINE ALOUD WITHOUT MAKING ANY MISTAKES. IF YOU MAKE A MISTAKE YOU MUST START AGAIN WITHOUT GOING ANY FURTHER.

THIS IS THIS PUZZLE
THIS IS IS PUZZLE
THIS IS HOW PUZZLE
THIS IS TO PUZZLE
THIS IS KEEP PUZZLE
THIS IS A PUZZLE
THIS IS DUMBO PUZZLE
THIS IS BUSY PUZZLE
THIS IS FOR PUZZLE
THIS IS FORTY PUZZLE
THIS IS SECONDS! PUZZLE

When your seat is at the back of the plane, and they run out of dinners just as they reach you.

WHAT ARE TWO THINGS YOU CAN NEVER EAT FOR DINNER?

"A good traveler has no fixed plans and is not intent on arriving." — Lao Tzu

M CE
M CE
M CE

BREAKFAST AND LUNCH; THREE
BLIND MICE.

Finding out that your plane is number 496 in the lineup to take off.

When you find that your connecting flight is on an 80-year-old two-seater "puddle- jumper."

WHAT GETS WETTER AND WETTER THE MORE IT DRIES?

I'M LIGHT AS A FEATHER, YET THE STRONGEST MAN CAN'T HOLD ME FOR MUCH MORE THAN A COUPLE OF MINUTES. WHAT AM I?

A TOWEL; HIS BREATH.

When the 400-pound man next to you falls asleep and leans on you.

WHAT IS ROUND AS A DISHPAN AND NO MATTER THE SIZE, ALL THE WATER IN THE OCEAN CAN'T FILL IT UP?

Lost Luggage

A young Filipino, traveling in Chicago, registered at the Hotel Sherman. Taking a walk, he became lost. He was ignorant of the name, location, and appearance of the hotel, and so was unable to find it again. Consequently, he selected another room in the Hotel Astor. Unwilling to acknowledge to the authorities that he was lost, he tried for five days to find the place where he had deposited his baggage.

Unsuccessful, he finally appealed to the authorities. The police soon found his original registration place, and informed him that for five days he had been living next door to the place he had left his baggage.

—From *Encyclopedia of 7,700 Illustrations* by Paul Lee Tan. 1979, (Rockville, Maryland: Assurance Publishers), pg. 1,216.

A SIEVE.

The captain drops the plane onto the runway from 60 feet.

The pilot who should have been a sports commentator.

WHAT OCCURS ONCE IN A MINUTE, TWICE IN A MOMENT, BUT NEVER IN AN HOUR?

YOU ARE IN A DARK ROOM WITH A CANDLE, A WOOD STOVE, AND A GAS LAMP. YOU ONLY HAVE ONE MATCH, SO WHAT DO YOU LIGHT FIRST?

THE LETTER M; THE MATCH.

98

The guy who takes off his shoes, bringing new meaning to the word "high" flier.

IMAGINE YOU ARE IN A SINKING ROWBOAT SURROUNDED BY SHARKS. YOU HAVE A HAMMER, SIX NAILS, AND A PLASTIC RAINCOAT. HOW WOULD YOU SURVIVE?

STOP IMAGINING.

Incorrect gate information.

The flight attendant who opens a can of soda and gives you a free shower.

WHAT HAPPENED IN 1961 AND WILL NOT HAPPEN AGAIN UNTIL 6009?

THE NUMBERS READ THE SAME UPSIDE-DOWN.

When the man next to you holds his paper so far over your side, you can't help but read it. Then he turns the page when you are in the middle of an article.

HOW COULD ALL OF YOUR COUSINS HAVE AN AUNT WHO IS NOT YOUR AUNT?

YOUR MOM IS THEIR AUNT.

Getting Off the Ground

I hope that this book made you smile. That's one of the reasons I wrote it. The second reason was to talk to you briefly about life's most important issue.

I guess most people say a prayer as they take off in a plane. Those who don't are probably at least "prayerful" when their plane hits severe turbulence. More than 90 percent of Americans believe in God, and most of them admit to praying each day.

Although I used to pray daily before I was a Christian, I didn't know God. If you had asked me if I was a good person, I would have said that I was. I would have said, "If there is a heaven, I will probably end up there because I'm not a bad person." But I was making a terrible mistake. God has a list of ten things we must do — they are called the Ten Commandments. In my ignorance, I didn't realize that I had already broken those Commandments and was in great danger.

The biblical explanation as to why each of us will die is because we have broken an uncompromising law. Just as we suffer the consequences of breaking the law of gravity if we jump out of a plane without a pararchute, so we will suffer the consequences of transgressing God's Moral Law. Let's see if you have broken this law (commonly referred to as the Ten Commandments):

1. Is God first in your life? Do you love Him with all of your heart, mind, soul, and strength? Do you love your neighbor as yourself? Does your love for your family seem like hatred compared to the love you have for the One who gave those loved ones to you?

2. Have you made a god in your own image, to suit yourself?

3. Have you ever used God's holy name in vain . . . substituting it for a four-lettered filth word to express disgust?

4. Have you kept the Sabbath holy?

5. Have you always honored your parents?

6. Have you hated anyone? Then the Bible says you are a murderer.

7. Have you had sex before marriage? Or have you lusted after another person? The Bible warns that you have committed adultery in your heart.

8. Have you ever stolen something? Then you are a thief.

9. If you have told even one lie, you are a liar and cannot enter the kingdom of God.

10. Finally, have you ever desired something that belonged to someone else? Then you have broken the Tenth Commandment.

Listen to your conscience. The Law leaves us all sinners in God's sight. On Judgment Day we will be found guilty, and end up in hell forever. Perhaps you are sorry for your sins, and you even confess them to God, but that doesn't mean that He will forgive you — no matter how sincere you are. Let me explain why. Imagine you are standing guilty in front of a judge. You face a $50,000 fine, and say, "Judge . . . I'm truly sorry for my crime." He would probably say, "So you should be! Now are you able to pay the $50,000 fine or not?" A judge must have grounds upon which he can release you. If I paid your fine, then you would be free from the demands of the law. That's precisely what God did in the person of Jesus Christ. Each of us stand guilty of breaking God's Law, but because Jesus paid our fine on the Cross 2,000 years ago, God can forgive us on the grounds of His suffering death. That's why you need Jesus Christ as your Savior. Without Him, the Law will send you to hell, and you will have no one to blame but yourself. God will make sure justice is carried out. The Bible says, "God commends His love toward us in that while we were yet sinners Christ died for us" (Rom. 5:8; NKJV). He gave His sinless life on the Cross, showing the depth of God's love for us. We broke God's Law — He paid the fine so that we could be free from its perfect demands. Then He rose from the dead and defeated the power of the grave.

If you repent, trust in the Savior, and obey His Word, God will forgive your sins and grant you everlasting life. The Bible says that all humanity is held captive to the fear of and power of death (Heb. 2:15). If you don't face your fear of death, then you will run from it until the day you die . . . and that day will come. The proof of your sin will be your death. Today, not only face the reality that you will die, but also do something about it — obey the gospel and live. Confess your sins to God, put your faith in Jesus Christ, then read the Bible daily and obey what you read. God will never let you down. Feel free to go to www.livingwaters.com and click on "Save Yourself Some Pain."

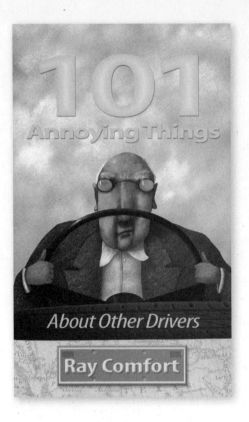

- *Filled with funny stories and "behind-the-wheel" encounters*
- *Presents a unique and entertaining "roadmap" to reach salvation*
- *Designed as an evangelism tool, it makes the perfect gift for friends, family,and co-workers*

Have you ever groaned in frustration at tailgaters (or been one yourself)? Or have you been frustrated by drivers who insist on putting on make-up,talking on their cell phones, and eating a four-course meal while driving? Evangelist Ray Comfort addresses these frustrations and many others in this hilarious book. Well-known apologist and evangelist Comfort has come up with over a hundred humorous jokes, stories, and encounters with other drivers this entertaining book. No more than two paragraphs each, these funny and light-hearted stories will bring a smile to your face. Humorous in content, but designed as an evangelizing tool, this fun book includes a salvation message. Through Comfort's encounters with "annoying drivers," he illustrates a simple and easy-to-understand gospel message for readers.

ISBN: 0-89221-668-9 • ISBN 13: 978-0-89221-668-0
176 pages • 5 1/4 x 8 3/8 • Trade Paper • Retail: $10.99
HUMOR / General